50 Effortless Cooking Dishes for Home

By: Kelly Johnson

Table of Contents

- Scrambled Eggs
- Hard-Boiled Eggs
- Fried Rice
- Grilled Cheese Sandwich
- Peanut Butter & Jelly Sandwich
- Avocado Toast
- BLT Sandwich
- Tuna Salad Sandwich
- Egg Salad Sandwich
- Simple Pancakes
- French Toast
- Oatmeal with Honey & Berries
- Yogurt Parfait with Granola
- Banana Smoothie
- Simple Green Salad
- Caesar Salad
- Cucumber & Tomato Salad
- Caprese Salad
- Chicken & Rice Bowl
- Spaghetti with Marinara Sauce
- Mac and Cheese
- Ramen with Egg & Vegetables
- Baked Potato with Sour Cream
- Mashed Potatoes
- Roasted Vegetables
- Grilled Chicken Breast
- Baked Salmon with Lemon
- Pan-Seared Steak
- Rice & Beans
- Garlic Butter Shrimp
- Simple Vegetable Stir-Fry
- Chicken Noodle Soup
- Tomato Soup with Grilled Cheese
- Vegetable Soup
- Baked Chicken Thighs

- Sheet Pan Sausage & Vegetables
- Sloppy Joes
- Tacos (Beef or Chicken)
- Quesadilla with Cheese & Veggies
- Guacamole with Tortilla Chips
- Hummus & Pita Bread
- Oven-Baked French Fries
- Cheeseburger with Classic Toppings
- Hot Dog with Ketchup & Mustard
- Baked Apples with Cinnamon
- Chocolate Mug Cake
- No-Bake Peanut Butter Bars
- Fruit Salad with Honey Drizzle
- Overnight Oats
- Simple Chocolate Chip Cookies

Scrambled Eggs

Ingredients:

- 2 eggs
- 1 tbsp butter
- 2 tbsp milk (optional)
- Salt & pepper to taste

Instructions:

1. In a bowl, whisk eggs, milk, salt, and pepper.
2. Melt butter in a pan over medium heat.
3. Pour in eggs and stir gently until just set.
4. Serve immediately.

Hard-Boiled Eggs

Ingredients:

- 2 eggs
- Water

Instructions:

1. Place eggs in a saucepan and cover with water.
2. Bring to a boil, then cover and remove from heat.
3. Let sit for 10–12 minutes, then transfer to an ice bath.
4. Peel and enjoy.

Fried Rice

Ingredients:

- 2 cups cooked rice (preferably day-old)
- 1 tbsp vegetable oil
- ½ cup diced carrots
- ½ cup frozen peas
- 2 eggs, beaten
- 2 tbsp soy sauce
- 1 tsp sesame oil
- 1 green onion, sliced
- 1 clove garlic, minced

Instructions:

1. Heat oil in a pan over medium heat.
2. Add carrots and cook for 2 minutes. Add garlic and peas, stirring for another minute.
3. Push veggies to one side, pour in beaten eggs, and scramble until cooked.
4. Stir in rice and soy sauce, cooking for 2–3 minutes.
5. Drizzle with sesame oil and garnish with green onions.

Grilled Cheese Sandwich

Ingredients:

- 2 slices bread
- 2 tbsp butter
- 2 slices cheddar cheese

Instructions:

1. Butter one side of each bread slice.
2. Place cheese between the unbuttered sides.
3. Grill on a pan over medium heat until golden brown on both sides.

Peanut Butter & Jelly Sandwich

Ingredients:

- 2 slices bread
- 2 tbsp peanut butter
- 2 tbsp jelly

Instructions:

1. Spread peanut butter on one slice of bread.
2. Spread jelly on the other slice.
3. Press together and serve.

Avocado Toast

Ingredients:

- 1 slice bread, toasted
- ½ avocado, mashed
- Salt & pepper to taste
- Red pepper flakes or sesame seeds (optional)

Instructions:

1. Spread mashed avocado over toast.
2. Season with salt, pepper, and toppings of choice.

BLT Sandwich

Ingredients:

- 2 slices bread
- 2 slices bacon, cooked
- 2 slices tomato
- 2 leaves lettuce
- 1 tbsp mayonnaise

Instructions:

1. Spread mayo on one side of each bread slice.
2. Layer bacon, lettuce, and tomato.
3. Press together and serve.

Tuna Salad Sandwich

Ingredients:

- 1 can tuna, drained
- 2 tbsp mayonnaise
- 1 tsp mustard
- ½ stalk celery, diced
- 1 tbsp lemon juice
- Salt & pepper to taste
- 2 slices bread

Instructions:

1. Mix tuna, mayo, mustard, celery, lemon juice, salt, and pepper.
2. Spread onto one slice of bread, top with another slice.

Egg Salad Sandwich

Ingredients:

- 2 hard-boiled eggs, chopped
- 2 tbsp mayonnaise
- ½ tsp mustard
- ½ stalk celery, diced
- Salt & pepper to taste
- 2 slices bread

Instructions:

1. Mix eggs, mayo, mustard, celery, salt, and pepper.
2. Spread onto one slice of bread and top with the other.

Simple Pancakes

Ingredients:

- 1 cup flour
- 1 tbsp sugar
- 1 tsp baking powder
- ½ tsp salt
- ¾ cup milk
- 1 egg
- 1 tbsp melted butter

Instructions:

1. Mix dry ingredients in a bowl.
2. Add milk, egg, and butter, stirring until smooth.
3. Cook in a buttered pan over medium heat, flipping when bubbles form.

French Toast

Ingredients:

- 2 slices bread
- 1 egg
- ¼ cup milk
- ½ tsp cinnamon
- ½ tsp vanilla extract
- 1 tbsp butter

Instructions:

1. Whisk egg, milk, cinnamon, and vanilla.
2. Dip bread into mixture, coating both sides.
3. Cook in a buttered pan over medium heat until golden brown.

Oatmeal with Honey & Berries

Ingredients:

- ½ cup rolled oats
- 1 cup milk or water
- 1 tbsp honey
- ¼ cup mixed berries

Instructions:

1. Cook oats with milk/water over medium heat until thickened.
2. Stir in honey and top with berries.

Yogurt Parfait with Granola

Ingredients:

- 1 cup Greek yogurt
- ½ cup granola
- ½ cup mixed berries (strawberries, blueberries, raspberries)
- 1 tbsp honey (optional)

Instructions:

1. In a glass or bowl, layer Greek yogurt, granola, and berries.
2. Drizzle with honey if desired.
3. Repeat layers and serve immediately.

Banana Smoothie

Ingredients:

- 1 banana
- 1 cup milk (or almond milk)
- ½ cup Greek yogurt
- 1 tbsp honey or maple syrup
- ½ tsp vanilla extract (optional)
- Ice cubes (optional)

Instructions:

1. Blend all ingredients until smooth.
2. Pour into a glass and enjoy!

Simple Green Salad

Ingredients:

- 4 cups mixed greens (lettuce, spinach, arugula)
- ½ cucumber, sliced
- ½ cup cherry tomatoes, halved
- ¼ red onion, thinly sliced
- 2 tbsp olive oil
- 1 tbsp balsamic vinegar
- Salt & pepper to taste

Instructions:

1. In a large bowl, toss greens, cucumber, tomatoes, and onion.
2. Drizzle with olive oil and balsamic vinegar.
3. Season with salt and pepper.

Caesar Salad

Ingredients:

- 4 cups romaine lettuce, chopped
- ½ cup croutons
- ¼ cup grated Parmesan cheese
- 3 tbsp Caesar dressing
- 1 grilled chicken breast (optional)

Instructions:

1. Toss romaine lettuce with Caesar dressing.
2. Top with croutons and Parmesan cheese.
3. Add grilled chicken if desired.

Cucumber & Tomato Salad

Ingredients:

- 1 cucumber, sliced
- 1 cup cherry tomatoes, halved
- ¼ red onion, thinly sliced
- 2 tbsp olive oil
- 1 tbsp lemon juice
- ½ tsp salt
- ¼ tsp black pepper

Instructions:

1. Mix cucumber, tomatoes, and onion in a bowl.
2. Drizzle with olive oil and lemon juice.
3. Season with salt and pepper.

Caprese Salad

Ingredients:

- 2 large tomatoes, sliced
- 8 oz fresh mozzarella, sliced
- ¼ cup fresh basil leaves
- 2 tbsp olive oil
- 1 tbsp balsamic glaze
- Salt & pepper to taste

Instructions:

1. Arrange tomato and mozzarella slices on a plate, alternating layers.
2. Sprinkle basil leaves over the top.
3. Drizzle with olive oil and balsamic glaze.
4. Season with salt and pepper.

Chicken & Rice Bowl

Ingredients:

- 1 cup cooked rice
- 1 grilled or baked chicken breast, sliced
- ½ cup steamed broccoli
- ¼ cup shredded carrots
- 1 tbsp soy sauce or teriyaki sauce

Instructions:

1. Place cooked rice in a bowl.
2. Top with sliced chicken, broccoli, and carrots.
3. Drizzle with soy sauce or teriyaki sauce.

Spaghetti with Marinara Sauce

Ingredients:

- 8 oz spaghetti
- 2 cups marinara sauce
- 1 tbsp olive oil
- 2 cloves garlic, minced
- ½ tsp red pepper flakes (optional)
- Salt & pepper to taste
- Grated Parmesan cheese (optional)

Instructions:

1. Cook spaghetti according to package instructions.
2. In a pan, heat olive oil and sauté garlic for 1 minute.
3. Add marinara sauce and simmer for 5 minutes.
4. Toss cooked pasta with the sauce.
5. Sprinkle with Parmesan cheese if desired.

Mac and Cheese

Ingredients:

- 8 oz elbow macaroni
- 2 tbsp butter
- 2 tbsp flour
- 1 cup milk
- 1 ½ cups shredded cheddar cheese
- Salt & pepper to taste

Instructions:

1. Cook macaroni according to package instructions.
2. In a saucepan, melt butter over medium heat. Stir in flour and cook for 1 minute.
3. Gradually whisk in milk and cook until thickened.
4. Stir in cheese until melted.
5. Mix in cooked macaroni and season with salt and pepper.

Ramen with Egg & Vegetables

Ingredients:

- 1 pack instant or fresh ramen noodles
- 2 cups water or broth
- 1 egg
- ½ cup mixed vegetables (mushrooms, spinach, carrots)
- 1 tbsp soy sauce
- ½ tsp sesame oil
- Green onions for garnish

Instructions:

1. Cook ramen noodles in boiling water or broth.
2. Add vegetables and cook for 2 minutes.
3. Crack an egg into the broth and let it poach for 2–3 minutes.
4. Stir in soy sauce and sesame oil.
5. Garnish with green onions and serve.

Baked Potato with Sour Cream

Ingredients:

- 1 large russet potato
- 1 tbsp olive oil
- ¼ tsp salt
- ¼ cup sour cream
- 1 tbsp chopped green onions

Instructions:

1. Preheat oven to 400°F (200°C).
2. Rub the potato with olive oil and salt.
3. Bake for 45–60 minutes until fork-tender.
4. Cut open and top with sour cream and green onions.

Mashed Potatoes

Ingredients:

- 4 medium potatoes, peeled and cubed
- ¼ cup butter
- ½ cup milk
- Salt & pepper to taste

Instructions:

1. Boil potatoes until fork-tender (about 15 minutes).
2. Drain and mash with butter and milk.
3. Season with salt and pepper.

Roasted Vegetables

Ingredients:

- 2 cups mixed vegetables (carrots, bell peppers, zucchini, broccoli)
- 2 tbsp olive oil
- 1 tsp salt
- ½ tsp black pepper
- ½ tsp garlic powder
- ½ tsp dried thyme or rosemary

Instructions:

1. Preheat oven to 400°F (200°C).
2. Toss vegetables with olive oil, salt, pepper, garlic powder, and thyme.
3. Spread on a baking sheet in a single layer.
4. Roast for 20-25 minutes, stirring halfway through.

Grilled Chicken Breast

Ingredients:

- 2 boneless, skinless chicken breasts
- 2 tbsp olive oil
- 1 tsp salt
- ½ tsp black pepper
- ½ tsp garlic powder
- ½ tsp paprika
- ½ tsp dried oregano or Italian seasoning

Instructions:

1. Preheat grill to medium-high heat.
2. Brush chicken with olive oil and season with spices.
3. Grill for 6-7 minutes per side or until internal temperature reaches 165°F (75°C).
4. Let rest for 5 minutes before slicing.

Baked Salmon with Lemon

Ingredients:

- 2 salmon fillets
- 1 tbsp olive oil
- 1 tbsp lemon juice
- 1 tsp salt
- ½ tsp black pepper
- ½ tsp garlic powder
- 2 lemon slices

Instructions:

1. Preheat oven to 400°F (200°C).
2. Place salmon fillets on a baking sheet lined with parchment paper.
3. Drizzle with olive oil and lemon juice, then season with salt, pepper, and garlic powder.
4. Place lemon slices on top and bake for 12-15 minutes.

Pan-Seared Steak

Ingredients:

- 1 steak (ribeye, sirloin, or filet)
- 1 tbsp butter
- 1 tbsp olive oil
- 1 tsp salt
- ½ tsp black pepper
- 2 garlic cloves, smashed
- 1 sprig fresh rosemary (optional)

Instructions:

1. Heat olive oil in a skillet over high heat.
2. Season steak with salt and pepper.
3. Sear for 2-3 minutes per side until browned.
4. Add butter, garlic, and rosemary, then baste the steak for another 1-2 minutes.
5. Remove and let rest for 5 minutes before slicing.

Rice & Beans

Ingredients:

- 1 cup cooked rice (white or brown)
- 1 can (15 oz) black or kidney beans, drained and rinsed
- 1 tbsp olive oil
- ½ onion, chopped
- 1 clove garlic, minced
- ½ tsp cumin
- ½ tsp paprika
- Salt & pepper to taste

Instructions:

1. Heat olive oil in a pan over medium heat.
2. Sauté onion and garlic until softened.
3. Add beans, cumin, paprika, salt, and pepper. Cook for 5 minutes.
4. Mix with cooked rice and serve.

Garlic Butter Shrimp

Ingredients:

- ½ lb shrimp, peeled and deveined
- 2 tbsp butter
- 2 cloves garlic, minced
- ½ tsp salt
- ¼ tsp black pepper
- ½ tsp red pepper flakes (optional)
- 1 tbsp lemon juice

Instructions:

1. Melt butter in a pan over medium heat.
2. Add garlic and cook for 30 seconds.
3. Add shrimp, salt, pepper, and red pepper flakes. Cook for 2-3 minutes per side.
4. Drizzle with lemon juice and serve.

Simple Vegetable Stir-Fry

Ingredients:

- 2 cups mixed vegetables (bell peppers, broccoli, carrots, snap peas)
- 1 tbsp vegetable oil
- 2 cloves garlic, minced
- 1 tbsp soy sauce
- ½ tsp ginger, grated
- ½ tsp sesame oil

Instructions:

1. Heat vegetable oil in a pan over medium-high heat.
2. Add garlic and ginger, then stir-fry for 30 seconds.
3. Add vegetables and cook for 5-7 minutes until tender.
4. Stir in soy sauce and sesame oil.

Chicken Noodle Soup

Ingredients:

- 1 tbsp olive oil
- ½ onion, chopped
- 2 carrots, sliced
- 2 celery stalks, chopped
- 2 cloves garlic, minced
- 6 cups chicken broth
- 2 cups shredded cooked chicken
- 1 cup egg noodles
- ½ tsp salt
- ¼ tsp black pepper
- ½ tsp dried thyme

Instructions:

1. Heat olive oil in a pot over medium heat.
2. Sauté onion, carrots, celery, and garlic for 5 minutes.
3. Add broth, chicken, salt, pepper, and thyme. Bring to a boil.
4. Add noodles and cook for 10 minutes.

Tomato Soup with Grilled Cheese

Ingredients:

- 1 tbsp olive oil
- ½ onion, chopped
- 2 cloves garlic, minced
- 1 can (28 oz) crushed tomatoes
- 2 cups vegetable broth
- 1 tsp sugar
- Salt & pepper to taste
- ½ cup heavy cream (optional)

Instructions:

1. Heat olive oil in a pot over medium heat.
2. Sauté onion and garlic until soft.
3. Add tomatoes, broth, sugar, salt, and pepper. Simmer for 10 minutes.
4. Blend until smooth and stir in heavy cream if using.

Grilled Cheese:

- 2 slices bread
- 2 slices cheese (cheddar or American)
- 1 tbsp butter

1. Butter both sides of bread and add cheese in between.
2. Cook on a skillet over medium heat until golden brown on both sides.

Vegetable Soup

Ingredients:

- 1 tbsp olive oil
- ½ onion, chopped
- 2 carrots, sliced
- 2 celery stalks, chopped
- 1 zucchini, diced
- 1 can (15 oz) diced tomatoes
- 4 cups vegetable broth
- 1 tsp salt
- ½ tsp black pepper
- ½ tsp dried basil

Instructions:

1. Heat olive oil in a pot over medium heat.
2. Sauté onion, carrots, and celery for 5 minutes.
3. Add zucchini, tomatoes, broth, salt, pepper, and basil. Simmer for 15 minutes.

Baked Chicken Thighs

Ingredients:

- 4 bone-in, skin-on chicken thighs
- 1 tbsp olive oil
- 1 tsp salt
- ½ tsp black pepper
- ½ tsp garlic powder
- ½ tsp paprika

Instructions:

1. Preheat oven to 400°F (200°C).
2. Rub chicken thighs with olive oil and season with spices.
3. Bake for 35-40 minutes until crispy and cooked through.

Sheet Pan Sausage & Vegetables

Ingredients:

- 4 sausage links (chicken, pork, or turkey)
- 2 cups mixed vegetables (bell peppers, zucchini, potatoes)
- 2 tbsp olive oil
- 1 tsp salt
- ½ tsp black pepper
- ½ tsp garlic powder

Instructions:

1. Preheat oven to 400°F (200°C).
2. Toss vegetables with olive oil and seasonings.
3. Spread sausage and vegetables on a sheet pan.
4. Bake for 25-30 minutes, stirring halfway through.

Sloppy Joes

Ingredients:

- 1 lb ground beef
- ½ onion, chopped
- 1 clove garlic, minced
- 1 cup tomato sauce
- 2 tbsp ketchup
- 1 tbsp Worcestershire sauce
- 1 tsp mustard
- ½ tsp salt
- ¼ tsp black pepper
- 4 hamburger buns

Instructions:

1. In a pan over medium heat, cook ground beef until browned. Drain excess fat.
2. Add onion and garlic, cooking until soft.
3. Stir in tomato sauce, ketchup, Worcestershire sauce, mustard, salt, and pepper. Simmer for 10 minutes.
4. Spoon mixture onto buns and serve.

Tacos (Beef or Chicken)

Ingredients:

- 1 lb ground beef or shredded chicken
- 1 tbsp olive oil
- 1 tsp chili powder
- ½ tsp cumin
- ½ tsp garlic powder
- ½ tsp paprika
- ½ tsp salt
- 8 small taco shells
- Toppings: shredded lettuce, diced tomatoes, shredded cheese, sour cream, salsa

Instructions:

1. Heat olive oil in a pan over medium heat.
2. Cook beef or chicken with spices until fully cooked.
3. Warm taco shells and fill with meat.
4. Add toppings of choice and serve.

Quesadilla with Cheese & Veggies

Ingredients:

- 2 flour tortillas
- 1 cup shredded cheese (cheddar, Monterey Jack, or mozzarella)
- ½ cup bell peppers, sliced
- ½ cup mushrooms, sliced
- ½ tsp olive oil

Instructions:

1. Heat olive oil in a pan over medium heat. Sauté bell peppers and mushrooms for 3 minutes.
2. Place one tortilla in the pan, add cheese and sautéed veggies, then top with another tortilla.
3. Cook for 2-3 minutes per side until golden brown.
4. Cut into wedges and serve.

Guacamole with Tortilla Chips

Ingredients:

- 2 ripe avocados
- 1 small tomato, diced
- ½ red onion, finely chopped
- 1 clove garlic, minced
- 1 tbsp lime juice
- ½ tsp salt
- ¼ tsp black pepper
- ¼ tsp cumin (optional)
- Tortilla chips for serving

Instructions:

1. Mash avocados in a bowl.
2. Stir in tomato, onion, garlic, lime juice, salt, pepper, and cumin.
3. Serve with tortilla chips.

Hummus & Pita Bread

Ingredients:

- 1 can (15 oz) chickpeas, drained
- 2 tbsp tahini
- 2 tbsp olive oil
- 1 clove garlic
- 1 tbsp lemon juice
- ½ tsp salt
- ¼ tsp cumin
- 2 tbsp water (as needed for consistency)
- Pita bread for serving

Instructions:

1. Blend chickpeas, tahini, olive oil, garlic, lemon juice, salt, and cumin in a food processor.
2. Add water as needed until smooth.
3. Serve with pita bread.

Oven-Baked French Fries

Ingredients:

- 2 large potatoes, cut into thin strips
- 1 tbsp olive oil
- ½ tsp salt
- ½ tsp paprika
- ¼ tsp black pepper

Instructions:

1. Preheat oven to 425°F (220°C).
2. Toss potatoes with olive oil, salt, paprika, and black pepper.
3. Spread on a baking sheet and bake for 25-30 minutes, flipping halfway through.

Cheeseburger with Classic Toppings

Ingredients:

- 1 lb ground beef
- ½ tsp salt
- ¼ tsp black pepper
- 4 slices cheese (cheddar, American, or Swiss)
- 4 burger buns
- Toppings: lettuce, tomato, pickles, ketchup, mustard, mayonnaise

Instructions:

1. Shape beef into 4 patties and season with salt and pepper.
2. Cook on a grill or stovetop over medium-high heat for 3-4 minutes per side.
3. Add cheese and let melt for 1 minute.
4. Toast buns and assemble burgers with toppings.

Hot Dog with Ketchup & Mustard

Ingredients:

- 4 hot dog buns
- 4 hot dogs
- Ketchup
- Mustard

Instructions:

1. Heat hot dogs on a grill, stovetop, or microwave until warm.
2. Place each hot dog in a bun.
3. Drizzle with ketchup and mustard. Serve immediately.

Baked Apples with Cinnamon

Ingredients:

- 2 apples, cored and sliced
- 1 tbsp butter, melted
- 1 tbsp brown sugar
- ½ tsp cinnamon
- ¼ tsp nutmeg (optional)

Instructions:

1. Preheat oven to 375°F (190°C).
2. Toss apple slices with melted butter, brown sugar, and cinnamon.
3. Spread on a baking sheet and bake for 20 minutes, or until soft.
4. Serve warm.

Chocolate Mug Cake

Ingredients:

- ¼ cup all-purpose flour
- 2 tbsp cocoa powder
- 2 tbsp sugar
- ¼ tsp baking powder
- Pinch of salt
- 3 tbsp milk
- 2 tbsp vegetable oil
- ¼ tsp vanilla extract

Instructions:

1. In a microwave-safe mug, mix flour, cocoa powder, sugar, baking powder, and salt.
2. Stir in milk, oil, and vanilla extract until smooth.
3. Microwave for 1-1½ minutes, until the cake rises and is set.
4. Let cool slightly and enjoy!

No-Bake Peanut Butter Bars

Ingredients:

- 1 cup peanut butter
- ½ cup honey
- 2 cups oats
- ½ cup chocolate chips (optional)

Instructions:

1. In a saucepan, heat peanut butter and honey over low heat until smooth.
2. Stir in oats and mix well.
3. Press into a parchment-lined baking dish.
4. Sprinkle chocolate chips on top (if using).
5. Refrigerate for 1 hour, then cut into bars.

Fruit Salad with Honey Drizzle

Ingredients:

- 1 cup strawberries, sliced
- 1 cup grapes, halved
- 1 cup pineapple, diced
- 1 cup blueberries
- 2 tbsp honey
- 1 tsp lemon juice

Instructions:

1. In a large bowl, combine all the fruit.
2. Mix honey and lemon juice in a small bowl.
3. Drizzle over the fruit and toss gently.
4. Serve chilled.

Overnight Oats

Ingredients:

- ½ cup rolled oats
- ½ cup milk (or almond milk)
- 1 tbsp chia seeds (optional)
- 1 tbsp honey or maple syrup
- ½ tsp vanilla extract
- ½ cup fruit (bananas, berries, or apples)

Instructions:

1. In a jar, mix oats, milk, chia seeds, honey, and vanilla extract.
2. Stir well, seal, and refrigerate overnight.
3. In the morning, top with fruit and enjoy!

Simple Chocolate Chip Cookies

Ingredients:

- ½ cup butter, softened
- ½ cup sugar
- ½ cup brown sugar
- 1 egg
- 1 tsp vanilla extract
- 1½ cups all-purpose flour
- ½ tsp baking soda
- ¼ tsp salt
- ¾ cup chocolate chips

Instructions:

1. Preheat oven to 350°F (175°C).
2. Cream together butter, sugar, and brown sugar.
3. Beat in egg and vanilla extract.
4. Mix in flour, baking soda, and salt until combined.
5. Fold in chocolate chips.
6. Drop spoonfuls onto a baking sheet and bake for 10-12 minutes.
7. Let cool and enjoy!